4

THE KEY

AND THE NAME OF THE KEY
IS WILLINGNESS

Copyright 1984 by Cheri Huber and June Shiver

ISBN13 978-0-9636255-4-0

Cover design by Marie Denkinger
sunwheelart@earthlink.net
Cover art by Sharon Williams

This printing 2014

These are some of the awarenesses that have been helpful to us in our practice. We are grateful for them and would like to share them with you.

The Key was originally handlettered. This edition is produced in a personal handlettering font. We chose this method so that this book can be read
> slowly with the heart
> instead of quickly with the head.

We offer this book in loving kindness.

For all who
follow this Path
and for all who are
approaching this Path

Please,
do not do yourself the disservice of assuming
there is something to do
that is more important
than just being

right here,
right now,
present,

aware,
attentive,
accepting.

We spend our lives trying to alter externals, trying to get what we want, trying to manipulate the "whats."

Relationships, friends, lovers, money, possessions, values, opinions, ideas, hopes, dreams, children, jobs, death, education, etc. are "WHATS."

Whats come and go.

Whats pass.

Whats are illusion.

Peace, joy, and freedom lie in
seeing the **process**,
not just the **content** of life.

We get so caught up in the specifics,
the "whats" of life, that we can't step back
and see the process, the broader view, the
whole.

We don't realize that
we experience our lives the way we do,
not because they actually are that way,
but because that's how we see them.

It's not what you do,

it's how you do it.

It's not what you see,

it's how you see it.

It's not what you think,

it's how you think it.

It's not what you feel,

it's how you feel it.

There is nothing wrong in the universe. Wrong exists only in our limited view.

Wrong (rong) adj. Not the way I want it
Right (rit) adj. How I think it should be
Fair (far) adj. What I want
Good (good) adj. What I like
Bad (bad) adj. What I don't like

These ideas we have about
how things are
and how they should be
exist only in our minds
and nowhere else!

That voice in your head is not
the voice of God.
It just sounds like it thinks it is.

Here's an exercise:

What are your definitions of the following words, not as defined by the dictionary or society, but as you honestly experience them?

wrong
right
fair
good
bad
honest
selfish
need
want
security
enough
loving
equal

Remember, these are <u>your</u> definitions.

Nothing needs to change.

You don't have to get better,
you already are better.
If you think you can do better,
do better.

Nothing real is stopping you.
the only thing stopping you
is the thought, the belief,
that something is stopping you.

What stops you is inside, not outside.

Love anything. Hate anything.
The effect you have on the thing you hate
might be negligible,
the effect on you,
monumental.

When you get through with all
this stuff,
all these problems
(job, education, husband, wife, house, children,
payments, bills, promises),
are you really going to be able to live?

This stuff,
these problems,
are your life.

When you get through with all this,
you'll be through with all this,

that's all.

We're going so fast all the time,
racing frantically toward a time
when we can

              S

                  L

                     O

                        W

                           down.

When we're going so frantically,
with so much to do and so little time,
it never occurs to us
that what we really need to do is

Stop believing that the treadmill

leads anywhere.

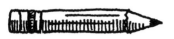

How do you:

slow down?

relax?

stop?

How do you keep yourself from:

slowing down?

relaxing?

stopping?

What kinds of things do you believe about life or about yourself that stop you from being the person you want to be?
What do you tell yourself about who you are or who you should be, and how does that get in your way?

Being the fastest, the richest, the thinnest, the smartest on the treadmill won't prove anything.

> There's nothing to prove,
> nothing to win,
> nothing to get.

What do you give up in order to fight this losing battle to be bigger, stronger, smarter, righter, perfecter?

> The fact that someone else is right
> doesn't mean you are wrong.
> Perhaps you are both right.
> Perhaps you are both wrong.
> Perhaps you are both right and wrong.

> If anyone loses,
> everyone loses.
> No one wins unless everyone wins.

No one,

no thing,

can take your peace,
your joy,
your adequacy,
away from you.

You have to give it up
voluntarily.

And we give it up so easily
for just about anything:

other people's opinions, late meals,
long lines, red lights...

What you want to become
is inside you.

And you are already responding to it

or you wouldn't be reading things like this.

The odds of anyone ever getting all
      or even most
of what s/he wants at any given time
      are very slim.

There are always
      irresponsible, late, rude, inept, stupid,
      uncooperative people;
a lack of
      parking places, appointments, money,
      promotions, weekends, dates, sex,
      affection;
an excess of
      criticism, judgments, things spilled
      on clothes, unexpected guests,
      red lights...

We have no choice about what we get.
We have absolute choice
                                    about what we do.

When we are trying to get what we want out of life

life can be very hard.

When we learn to want what we get in our lives

life can be very easy.

Instead of the common
"I want what I want when I want it,"
we learn to say,
"I want what I get when I get it."

I might not always like it,
but I can always accept it.

What kinds of things do you give up your peace and joy for? Consider lifetime "whats" such as job and family; current whats such as specific people or causes; cosmic whats such as death or religion; and everyday whats such as the store you are hurrying to is closed or you just spilled something on your favorite pants. Make a list if you would like.

How do you determine what you want?

How do you feel and act when you get what you want?

How do you feel and act when you don't get what you want?

What do you give up in order to cling to your notions about what you want?

IT IS EASIER
TO WANT WHAT YOU GET
THAN TO
GET WHAT YOU WANT.

When you want what you get,
you have always got what you want,
because you have always got what you get.

This is not to say
that we shouldn't have or do.

Remember:
There is no reason to do or not to do, to
have or not to have, anything. It is the
process, the how, we are concerned with, not
the content, the whats.

The process of "wanting"
is different from
the processes of "having" and "doing."

It seems that wanting results in having or
doing. When we look more closely we see
that wanting only results in more wanting,
in the increasingly demanding
habit of wanting.

Having or doing the object of wanting
satisfies only briefly and then
the wanting recaptures our attention.

These are the four causes of suffering:
- not getting what you want
- getting what you want and not being
  satisfied with it
- being separated from those or that
  which you love
- having to endure the presence of
  those or that which you do
  not love

These four all come down
to the same thing:
not getting what you want.

We think that wanting is the source of our
satisfaction.

                    In fact, it is the
source of our dissatisfaction.

   One process does not lead to another.
       Wanting does not lead to having.
       Wanting leads to wanting.
       Having leads to having.
       Doing leads to doing.
       Being leads to being.
   Dissatisfaction leads to dissatisfaction.

It is very important that we learn
          how "wanting" happens
          rather than believing
          we must get what we want.

First, find the contentment,
             the joy,
             the peace where you are.

To want is to believe that you are
      lacking, inadequate.
The present moment lacks nothing.
The present moment is all that is.

First, experience what is,
                    what actually is,
not assuming there's a lack,
then decide what, if anything,
you could want.

What is, IS.

Could be, should be, ought to be,
might be, hope will be,
wish could be, want to be,
are postures we maintain
to avoid accepting what is,

to remain ignorant,
or ignore-ant,
of what is.

In this way we manage to avoid
the only time in which we live.

Our lives consist of
WHAT IS
in the present moment.

Nothing but the way it is
could ever be,
or
should ever be.

"Should" is a stick we use
to beat ourselves with.

THIS IS IT.

Anything else is just our
      "better idea."

There is nothing wrong with the universe.

The only "wrong" is in our thinking,
in our believing

in our better idea.

"Should"

is

illusion

fantasizing.

"Should" is "Never Never Land."
Should never has been
and never will be.

When we stop comparing what is right here
and right now with what we wish were,
we can begin to enjoy what is.
(We might as well enjoy it;

it's all we've got.)

And we don't really know for sure that we
don't want it
because we've never fully experienced it,
we've always been off
looking at how we'd rather life were.

If this is all we've got,
it's also the best we've got.

Why not enjoy it?

Remember,
just because you don't like something
doesn't mean there is something
wrong with it.

It just means you don't like it.

A little secret between us:
Regardless of what someone might think
about what IS,

it is perfect.

Until we learn to accept,
we cling to things being
    the way they have been,
    or we wish they were,
    or want them to be,
    or hope they will be.
We tense our muscles,
dig in our heels,
and RESIST.

Then we believe the energy we have put into resisting change is actually maintaining the status quo.

We begin to believe that we
are holding things together.
Then we conclude: I am in control.
This conclusion is an illusion.

When we learn to accept everything

that comes into our lives,

we are free from the pain

and suffering of resistance.

Resistance does not work.
We have two choices.

#1. We can accept
     what is.

#2. We can resist
     what is.

Results of our choice:
#1. none
#2. none, except suffering

In acceptance there is peace.
In resistance there is suffering.
The choice is always ours.
It is just that simple.
And no one ever said it was easy.

What are you resisting in your life?

You,
each moment,
contain all that is,
everything you seek.

When you know that,
you see perfection and complete adequacy
all around you.

When you don't know that,
you spend all your time
trying to manipulate externals
so that you can get what you think
you need to make you feel "enough."*

*In Zen, this is known as adding legs to a snake, or
putting another head on the one you already have.

It is not necessary, or desirable,
to try to become someone
you think is better than
the way you are.

Just be willing to find out
who and how you really are.

You might be surprised to find
that when you let yourself be
who you really are,
not who you think you are,
or who you're afraid you are,
you are quite an acceptable person.

And with a little practice, you'll even realize
that you are, in fact,
a love-able person.

— 🧸 —

The ways you think you are,
not the ways you really are,
are the bars on your own
personal prison.

Please recall:

Just because you think something is so
(that you are bad, selfish, ugly, brilliant,
superior, inadequate)

doesn't mean it's so.

It just means you think it's so.

You are doing your life.

It's not that you are responsible for it in
the sense that you are to blame or that
you cause what happens in your life.

It's just that your
feelings, reactions, thoughts, attitudes,
theories, standards, beliefs, likes, dislikes,
wants, needs... are **yours.**

They create your world.
They are what you call "I" or "me."

And it this whole person
that you must face honestly
and learn to love and accept
through compassion.

When we waste all our time
trying to be better,
trying to improve ourselves,
we're failing to make the only contribution
we'll ever be qualified to make:
our own.

You don't have to change anything,
especially yourself.

You are the most perfect (and only) you
ever produced.
Be content with that.

Idealizing about the perfect you
just wastes your precious opportunity

for a perfect NOW.

Sit back, close your eyes and let an image come to you of your "perfect self," the idealized you you wish you were or think you "should" be. Picture what you and your life would be like.

PERFECT ME

Now let an image come to you that represents your "worst self," the way you see yourself when you are awful. Picture yourself as the person you "should not" be.

AWFUL ME

We maintain by resisting.
We maintain who we <u>think</u> we are
by resisting who we <u>really</u> are.

The more I try to become a better person,
the more I resist who I am,
the more I stay stuck where I am.

When I say YES,
when I embrace however I am,
I've already changed.

The moment I let go, everything is different,
though probably nothing external changed.
(Consider where the change actually occurred.
All I did was let go of my resistance.)

If you can't say YES, try OKAY.
It's a beginning.

Now, take a couple of deep breaths and let an image come to you that reflects as clearly as possible how you really are. See yourself going about your daily life, doing what you do, thinking your thoughts, feeling your feelings...

REALLY ME

Can you picture what your life would be like
if you accepted* it (if you loved it) as it is?

Picture of my life
accepted as it is.

*Remember, acceptance is not resignation.

Resignation happens
    with your head
                d

            o

                w

                    n.

Acceptance happens
    with your head u
                        p.

When you start being too successful,
    doing too well,
    getting too good
    at this process of letting go,
there's a good chance you'll lose interest.

Because if you really let go,
    if you really accept,
        you're going to change.

And there's a good chance
that's the last thing you <u>really</u> want to do.

Why?
When you let go in the way we are talking
about, a little gap is left in your identity, in
who you think you are. And even though we
say we want to be different, when we
actually begin to change, we often get pretty
scared, and that's okay, too.

SAY YES!

SIMPLY MEET EACH EXPERIENCE OF LIFE,
INSIDE AND OUT,
BODY, FEELINGS AND MIND,
WITH ALL THE LOVE AND ACCEPTANCE
YOU CAN MUSTER.

If you feel like you could love more,
love more.

If you think you would like to work
on your reactions,
  appreciate yourself for being willing,
   be grateful for the awareness,
    and love yourself for caring.

Peace and joy are what is left
when we stop doing
everything else.

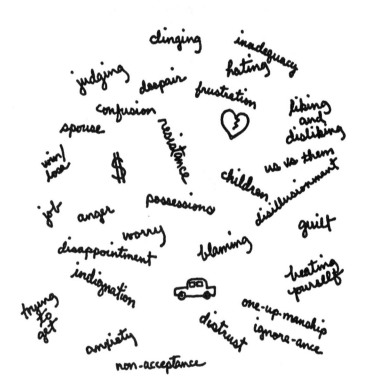

"Then why do we keep doing those things?"

There is surely a payoff for maintaining life as we know it (especially the horrors, the shocking awfulnesses of the world).

What would we talk about without them? What would be the daily news?

Wanting always to be
 right, good, strong,
 smart, successful,
 loving, rich

is like wanting always to have
 summer,
 daytime, sunshine,
 warmth, and 70°.

 Not only is it impossible,
 it's boring.

Until we have accepted where we are in our growth,
>we can't go anywhere else.

(As long as we are trying to get rid of something, we are ensuring that it will stay with us.)

When we accept where we are, we are capable of anything (we are all-potential).
We are no longer driven to be only one way: good, right, smart, strong...

We can love ourselves when we are
>wrong as well as right,
>weak as well as strong,
>angry as well as peaceful.

And this is good, because there is no such thing as a one-sided coin.

A wise little secret:

You do not need to know anything
in order to be wise.
All you need to do to be wise is to accept.

You don't need to have anything
"figured out" or "together."

Love as much as you can
from where you are
with what you've got.
That's the best you can ever do.

Remember: It's the process,
not the content,
that counts.

Total love and acceptance
is the wisest thing you can do.

It does no good
            to search frantically for peace,
to seek anxiously after love, joy or freedom.

If you want joy, be joyful.
If you want peace, be peaceful.

        It is good to be a person of means.
            If the end is never in sight,
                it doesn't matter.

We do what we do for the joy of doing, not
because we're going to get a reward when
it's over.*

*If we're doing what we're doing to get a
reward, the odds are real good that we'll be
disappointed a lot.

We know what's right. We don't know what's right for everyone or everything (though sometimes we act as if we think we do). It's not necessary or desirable to know everything, or anything, for everybody.

You know what's right for you each moment.
Not necessarily fun or pleasurable--
just right.
Deep down in your bones,
in your muscles, in your insides,
in your heart.

It might take some practice before you trust you have that knowingness, but if you pay attention, you will see that it is already guiding you through life. To the degree that you know it, do it. Not because you should, but because it feels good to do what you know is right!

Recall times when you knew in your heart
what to do but didn't do it, times when you
followed your head.

                    How did you feel?

Recall times when you listened to your
intuitive knowing and followed the guidance of
your heart.

                    How did you feel?

Do you experience a difference between
making a decision intuitively (heart) and
rationally (head)?   If so, what is that
difference like for you?

Here's a magic formula:

To prove to yourself
that you are a good person
who doesn't need to be punished,
choose to do what you know is right.

If you want to continue to be unhappy,
grab for the fleeting moments
of whatever your heart is telling you
aren't right for you
so you can continue to see yourself
as a bad person.

When you are unhappy
about something you have done, it's probably
not because of what you have done
so much as that you did not listen
to your heart
when it guided you not to do it.

Just do what you know is right.

You can do it for yourself
and as a gift for everyone else.

Do good
and feel good
and be happier
and more willing
and more loving
and more forgiving
and more accepting
and more compassionate
and the whole world will feel better.

When we are willing to let ourselves feel
good, when we are ready to forgive ourselves
for ancient crimes and sins,
                        real and imagined,
we begin to choose to do that which lets us
feel good about ourselves.

        We do this not because we "should."
          We do it because it feels good,
                because we want to.

You see, when it comes right down to it,
it doesn't really matter to us
what others think of us.
                        They criticize us
and we're defensive; they compliment us and
we don't believe them.

    The only praise or blame we really accept
                is from ourselves.

Exercises:

1. Do a kindness for someone* every day for a week.

2. Each night before going to sleep, take ten minutes and remember all the kind things you did that day.** Include smiles, compliments, kind words and thoughts...

3. Make recordings of the kindnesses you do and listen to them often.

* Remember, you are a someone!

** If you hear a voice inside saying that you are not a kind person, consider this: would someone who loves you and is on your side be so unkind as to say that to you?

Freedom lies in seeing
        how we do liking and disliking,

not in getting
all the things we like

or in getting rid of
all the things we dislike.

If you find something unacceptable,
draw a bigger circle of acceptance.

Just keep drawing a bigger circle
until nothing is excluded.

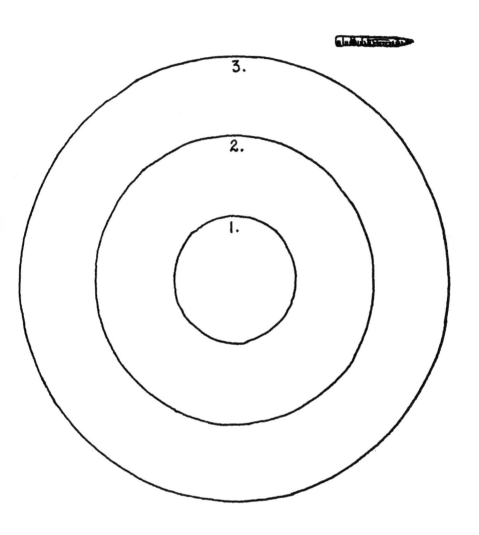

3.

2.

1.

Consider what you can accept easily (1), what you are working on accepting (2), and what still seems completely unacceptable (3).

What I am currently* experiencing as unacceptable is:

*Check back in six months or a year and see if all these "unacceptables" are still unacceptable or if some of them are inside the circle of acceptance.

Remember:

You don't have to give up
        the unacceptables--

you'll just suffer
        with each one you cling to.

("Pushing away" and "holding on to" are two
sides of the same coin. They are both
"clinging.")

        And we do suffer
        with each one we cling to.

Don't waste your time trying to change
anything.

(You don't even know
who wants to change or what you would
change or what the change would bring.
You'd just be trading one opinion for
another.)

Just draw a circle of acceptance
around everything in your awareness.
Just say YES.

You don't have to do anything about anything.
Just let everything be as it is,
(it is anyway),
at least until you see how you're doing it.

If you think you can feel better
        by doing something else
        or being something else
        or being somewhere else,
        then
        feel better.

Don't be confused that you really need to
        do something else
        or be something else
        or be somewhere else.

        Just be content
        to feel better.*

*This can save a great deal of time, energy,
and money.

Whether life is seen
as an opportunity
or a burden
depends on one's point of view,
not on one's circumstances.

You have learned
to walk,
to talk,
to dress yourself,
to drive a car,
to prepare food,
to play a musical instrument (?),
to speak another language (?),
to do all sorts of things that
in the beginning seemed insurmountable.

Because you wanted to.

If you see a problem, it's yours.
If you think somebody should do something,
remember that you are a somebody.

Be what you want the world to be.

Stop fighting.
You are the only one
standing between you
and peace.

When you can let things be as they are,
and not how you've decided they should be,
you can begin to see that the only thing
making you unhappy

is your "better idea."

Once you see that your better idea
is not better for anyone
but you,
you can begin to see other views,
then all views,
then what "views" really are.

All that is required
is that you accept
that which is totally unacceptable
to you.

(There's a clue there. It says "to you." Not
to everybody. Not to the world or society.
Not to God. To you.)

That which is unacceptable to you
exists only through the power you give it.

If you stop making it a problem,
it ceases to be a problem.

All you must do
is accept all
that is unacceptable
to you.

We
push
our
own

buttons.

In learning to take responsibility for our experience, our language misleads us because we say:
"He is handsome."
"The sunset is beautiful."
"She is angry."
rather than:
"My experience of him is 'handsome'."
"My experience of the sunset is 'beautiful'."
"My experience of her is 'angry'."

Is that always true? Can't I ever experience something that isn't a part of me, that isn't "mine"?

Yes, it is always true.
No, we can't experience something that isn't a part of ourselves.

It is helpful when learning to take responsibility to realize that our difficulties lie with our experience, not with externals.

We want the externals
to be the cause
of who we are.

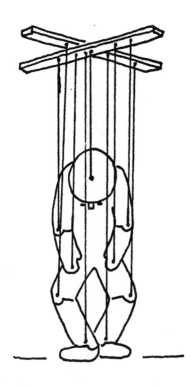

In fact, the externals
are the result
of who we are.

Seeing oneself as a victim is a choice,
not a requirement.

At any time, one can choose to be

FREE!

CLICK

The entire world is a mirror.
The entire world is a mirror.

THE ONLY THING
YOU CAN EVER EXPERIENCE
IS YOURSELF.

You think your thoughts, feel your feelings, experience your experience. You never experience anyone else's. Everything you think, feel, do, see is you.

Your thoughts, feelings, ideas, values, philosophies, opinions, "create" your world.

Everything you experience is as it is because that's how you experience it.

PROJECTION

or
How We Create the World We See

We experience the world the way we do because of who we are, not because of how it is. We project our thoughts, feelings, values, etc., onto everything. If we are unaware of this fact, we believe that what we see is true "out there."

Well, our projections at any given time might or might not be true for whatever we're projecting onto, BUT IT IS ALWAYS TRUE FOR THE PERSON SEEING IT. (Notice whose head it appeared in and whose mouth it came out of.)

Also, we tend to "give away" negative qualities and feel better, while we "give away" positive qualities and feel lacking.

Once you know that what you are
experiencing is the result of how you are,
                of how you see the world;
you will be less involved with trying to change
the content of your experience.

    You live in the world you have chosen.

    Your world continues to be the same,
  not because that's the way the world is,
          but because you continue
          to make the same choices.

Any time we attempt to cling
to one side of a duality,
we are clinging equally to its opposite.
(Clinging and pushing away are the same.)

We hold onto someone we love,
and they leave us.
We try to push something away,
and we can't get rid of it.
We want only quiet, refined, intelligent
people around us. We are plagued by
loud, ignorant, rude people.

Our standards have "created" both groups.

When we accept that both simply are
sometimes this,
sometimes that,
we are free.

What you see
is who you are.*

* This glass is
  □ half full
  □ half empty

Anything that happens could be experienced
in millions of ways.

What happens is not important.
How we react to what happens
is very important

It is not what we get that matters,
it is what we do that matters.

We can let go any time we are willing.

There is no way to _get_ love
or peace or joy or freedom.
To _be_ love-joy-peace-freedom
is the way.

The process, the means, is the point,
not the end.

If we really want to live differently, we are
going to have to find the willingness to stop
allowing self-hate (see page 88)
to punish,
  criticize,
    judge,
      beat,
        and otherwise "improve" us.

The way out of this mess we are in is
directly though the center.

We are free
the moment we are willing
to accept ALL.

No resistance at all to anything,
including our own thoughts and feelings.

What is, is.

Growing up, we are conditioned to believe that we can be improved by a very cruel system of rejection and abuse.

We call this cruel system egocentric karmic conditioning/self-hate.

Its slogan is
"Building a Better World through Hatred."

Its motto is
"You, too, can hate yourself into being a better person."

But the fact is that "you" are not hating "yourself."

You are being hated and beaten by egocentric karmic conditioning/self-hate, and that will never "make you a better person"!

Nothing real in the universe requires you to hate.

Nothing real punishes, rejects, or is cruel to you or anyone else.

Allowing self-hate to beat and punish you is what keeps you from seeing that there is no such thing as a person that needs to be beaten!

But we've been taught to believe that submitting to self-hate's beatings is the good and right person thing to do,

which is not true.

Submitting to the beatings just reinforces egocentric karmic conditioning/self-hate!

Would you teach a child to love
by hating, beating, and rejecting it
or by lovingly guiding it
to experience its inherent goodness?

We are all children and we can find our own
inherent goodness--the goodness that IS us--

through lovingkindness.

Exercise:

Circumstances have made it necessary for you to be responsible for a newborn baby. Consider how you would like that baby to be, how you want him/her to grow up, what kind of adult you would like him/her to be.
Consider all the things you will do and ways you will be in order to provide the best life experience for the baby.

Now begin to do those things for yourself!

It seems that we are stuck
with needing to take responsibility
for being loving and accepting

even of ourselves.

Perhaps if we stopped allowing self-hate to beat us there would be no reason to continue the behavior that "leads" to the beating. For example, if you stopped letting self-hate beat you for overeating, would you still overeat? Please don't be too quick to believe that you would eat everything in sight. You believe it, but that doesn't mean it's true.

Find out. The worst that could happen is that you would overeat and then go on a diet and lose the weight, and you know how to do that. And maybe, just maybe, when you start to love, support, and care for yourself --not in an egocentric sense but just as a basically kind, caring, decent person--you won't want to hurt your body anymore. Maybe you won't let self-hate beat you or suffer by feeling inadequate and unattractive.

Feeling better about yourself
through compassion and acceptance
truly is not egocentric.

It's the first giant step
                    away from egocentricity.

        Being kind to yourself
            lets you be kinder to others--
and that just might be
the finest gift
you can give the world.

Egocentricity
or self-indulgence
or selfishness
means satisfying one small part of yourself
whose desire is temporary and fleeting.

It is possible to do
what is most compassionate for all
the parts of yourself.

Not indulging yourself doesn't mean never
having an ice cream cone
or a new car.

It means not always having an ice cream
cone or a new car every time you want one.

There is a middle way that transcends
always and never.

We continue to choose our old ways,
the ways that cause us to suffer
because they're familiar,
safe and comfortable.

We know how to do that,
and we know who we are when we're doing it.

No risks here.

Many of us have to be very miserable
before we'll risk the insecurity
of doing something different,
of going against our conditioning,
of letting go of our ideas
about how life "should" be.

We find our willingness
to let go
when we have suffered enough.

We suffer because we cling.
Suffering is caused by our unwillingness
to accept what IS.

(And that's okay. Not having suffered enough
is not a reason to beat yourself.)

   We suffer when:
      We don't get what we want.
      We get what we want and are
         not satisfied with it.
      We are separated from those
         or that which we love.
      We must endure the presence
         of those or that which we
         do not love.

When we see that the world we experience
is created by our own projections and
postures, we realize there is **nothing** out
there to hold on to. If we believe there is,
we have bought a bill of goods.

Getting everything in the world
doesn't protect us from suffering.
It could all be gone tomorrow. Today even.

And just because you know this
doesn't mean you are any less safe
than you ever were.
Now you can see how it is.
No more reason to try to kid yourself.
Might as well relax. Might as well let go.

Nothing will be any worse,
and it just might be
a whole lot better!

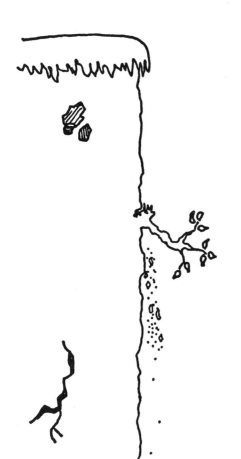

Just let go and fall...
UP!

There is no reason not to have it all.

You need not waste your time
        trying to get rid of
what you don't want in your life.

Just add what you do want.

If you think you'll be happier
        if you are single or
        if you have a new Rolls Royce,
            then
        BE HAPPIER!

Don't waste your time
        trying to get rid of your mate
        or trying to get a new car.

Add what you really want--
HAPPIER.

Our relationships with others
are based on liking and disliking.
(More on disliking, it would seem, since, of
the people you have met in your life, there
are many more who are not still around
than who are.)
We look for the things
we <u>don't</u> like about everything.
How it is different from me.
How it is "other."
How we are separate.

"Oh, I'm not like that." "I would never do
that." "I don't know how people can be like
that!" (Sure I do. I'm seeing it, aren't I?)

The obvious conclusion of my judgments is
that my way is better.
I am different, better, superior.
And that separation causes my suffering.

There is no reason,
no need,
to make a contest out of anything.

It is not necessary to demand
that life be a certain way
and then be unhappy
when it's not.
It is not necessary
to be frustrated or angry
or anxious or tense.
People are,
but they don't have to be.

Unhappiness is not a requirement.
Unhappiness is the result of wanting
something other than what is.

And if you find yourself suffering
because you've got something
you don't want...

if you can feel compassion for yourself
for suffering,
you will cease to suffer.

When you love yourself in your unhappiness,
you are no longer suffering,
you are loving.
We are not suffering when we are loving.

Remember, JOY travels from the inside
to the outside.

Look for the joy

in every moment.

Exercise:
See if you can find joy in doing something you
have told yourself is awful.

The problem is not with the "what,"
       the thing,
       the external.
The problem is with us,
       with our own process
       of liking and disliking.

We literally like and dislike ourselves to death. (Stress is liking and disliking.)

If you have to eat custard, and custard is your very favorite thing in the world, you're in heaven, you're ecstatic.
If you have to eat custard and you hate custard, despise it worse than anything, you're in hell, you're miserable.

The problem is not with the custard.

It is much easier to see that with custard
than it is with the boss,
                    husband/wife,
                    in-laws,
                    government, etc.,
and no less true.

        Suffering is not a requirement.
        Letting go of liking/disliking
            is not a requirement.
        It is simply a way to end suffering.

And you can know that as long as you cling to
a fixed idea of how life needs to be,
                    you are bound to suffer.

Because much of the time
        life just won't be the way
                    you want it to be.

Everything changes.
Suffering is the result of clinging
in an attempt to resist
change.

When we comprehend the process
of suffering,
how we do suffering,
we are free to choose not to do it anymore.

To do anything
there must be the willingness
to do it.
Achievement
is commensurate with effort.
Effort is commensurate
with willingness.

And the only thing standing in your way is
the "what" you have decided is in your way,
the "what" you are seeing as in your way,
the "what" you believe is in your way.

If you didn't experience it as an
////////obstacle,
would it be one?

What are you experiencing as an obstacle in your life?

What belief are you clinging to about how life should be that makes this an obstacle?

What have you already decided about this obstacle (its future, how things are going to be, etc.)?

What are you getting out of having this obstacle in your life--positive and negative?

What would happen if you let go?

This little quiz is a formula you can use to work on any problem.

Given a choice, we will almost always choose
our conditioned habits
over
what we know is best for us.

For instance,
I want to quit smoking,
but it feels so uncomfortable when I stop.
I want to meditate,
but my thoughts drive me crazy when I sit.
I want not to drink,
but friends put so much pressure on me.
I want to be vegetarian,
but the carnivore in me screams NO.

It is good to remember
that no one
ever died
of uncomfortable.

We always do
what we are willing to do.

We always have a choice.
"I can't," is what we say
in order to keep pretending
that we are not responsible.

Here is a definition of perfect trust:
  We always do what we want to do.

When we start to use words like "I choose"
and "I choose not," we start to be
honest with ourselves.

Think of three things you can't do. It is helpful to keep this within the realm of possibility--not "I can't flap my wings and fly."

1.

2.

3.

Now repeat the same three with
"I won't..."

1.

2.

3

Now, the same three with
"I choose not..."

1.

2.

3.

This is your best opportunity...

There will never be
a better opportunity than this one.
No better time, no better place,
no better circumstance.

Right here. Right now. Right this minute.

If it's really a hard time for you,
you're closest to the truth.
When you are drowning,
that is your best opportunity
to learn to swim!
Why? Because there is nothing else on your
mind, nothing you need to get done first. It
is your first priority.

And we always do what is truly
our first priority.

Do not be confused by what you say
is most important to you.

Watch what you do.

What you do
is what is most important to you.

If the answers were in
the places you've been looking...

you would already
have found them.

Obviously,
   if your life were completely happy,
   you wouldn't still be looking for answers.

And yet our fear
   of doing something differently,
   of facing the unknown,
   of going against society's norms,
   of questioning our conditioning
is so great that we continue to follow the
same patterns over and over,
even when we know
full-well
         that they lead to unhappiness.

We continue to choose our beliefs
over our experience.

A rat in a laboratory learns very quickly not
to go down the tunnel if there is no longer
cheese at the other end.

A human being will continue to go down the
tunnel even though **there never has been
any cheese at the end!**

We can learn as much from what we
reject
as from what we
accept.

What you are pushing away
might contain exactly the clue
you have been looking for.

In other words...

if the answers you are seeking
were in the places you have been looking,
you would already have found them.

Our defenses
don't prove we need to be defended,
they prove we are not
                  taking care of ourselves.
They prove we are not giving ourselves the
love, compassion and care we need.

And the absence of that love, compassion
and care makes us feel very vulnerable.

We have identified with a small,
separate self who suffers and we
have forgotten that is not
                  who we really are.

That which you are seeking
is causing you to seek.

As long as you are looking outward,
you are looking in the wrong direction.

This is an equal opportunity life.

We each have all we need

each moment.

We can choose
to let go

and be free...

When we begin to take responsibility, we are like the conductor of a large symphony orchestra. The various instruments are the parts of us, all our ways of being, our needs, wants, moods, etc. The symphony is our life.

Sometimes we see parts of ourselves that we decide are bad, wrong, and undesirable and that should be gotten rid of. This is like having the string section hear the cymbals and say, "Oh, no, that sounds awful! We've got to get rid of that noise! All we need are stringed instruments because they sound so beautiful." (Beauty clearly being in the ear of the beholder.)

But an orchestra made up of only stringed instruments would be lacking, incomplete. It could make many beautiful sounds, but it couldn't make all music. Only one section of instruments could hate another. The conductor can hear the beauty in all and knows that each is essential to the whole.

When we need a drum roll in life,
a violin simply won't do!

So even though we were taught to believe
we need to hold onto **this**
and push **that** away,

it is simply not true.

When we hear all the instruments playing together in harmony, we will be very grateful that we could not get rid of even the smallest, apparently most insignificant, piece.

Our lives can be different
in any moment we choose
to change our choices.

When we are too busy to pay attention,
we are choosing ignorance.

Practice...*

If you want to call yourself a tennis player,
you can borrow a racket and a few balls and
go out and hit the balls
with the racket.

If you want to play
tennis, you buy a racket, take some lessons,
and play when you have time.

If you want to play tennis well, you find a
teacher, take lessons, practice, and play
regularly.

If you want to be a master tennis player,
you find a teacher, absorb every bit of
guidance, practice every possible moment, and
devote your entire life to your training.

⇨

Our lives are as they are
because we choose them.

We want to say, "Oh, but I don't have time
to pay attention. I'm too busy to be aware."
That's okay.
It's just good to know
who is making the decisions.

Your life is not beyond you.

*And remember, practice only when you
want to, not because you "should."

Not to worry...
There is nothing to worry about.
   No urgency.
   No hurry.
When you are tired enough of struggling,
      of suffering, of being unhappy,
                  you'll stop.

One day you'll be different.
It will be like walking around a corner
         or turning on a light.
   Everything will be different
   and nothing will have changed.

Someday you'll do it.
   When you're tried enough
      of struggling
      of suffering
      of being unhappy...
            or you could just do it now.

HOW

How do you do it?
How do you let go?
How do you accept?
How do you stop suffering?
How do you find compassion?
How do you learn to love?
      HOW?????

How did you learn to walk?
Did someone tell you about the
   muscles and bones and tendons and
   blood in your legs?
Did someone explain how the muscles
   in your torso and arms and legs
   work together, and how
   messages come into and go out of
   your brain, and how...

Or did you one day decide that you wanted to get up and go so badly
that nothing could stop you.

Not fear or pain or ignorance or insecurity. You wanted to walk and the only way to do it was to get up

and do it.

That's how.

(Continued on page 1)

TALK WITH CHERI

"Open Air" Radio Show

Open Air is Cheri's interactive, internet-based call-in radio show.
Call in and talk, or just listen, and find access to archived shows at
www.openairwithcherihuber.org

Online Classes

Cheri conducts interactive online classes via e-mail
on a wide variety of subjects
related to Zen Awareness Practice.
To be notified of future classes
sign up at www.livingcompassion.org.

Books and Recordings

All Cheri Huber titles are available from your local
independent bookstore or online at www.livingcompassion.org.
Also available online are MP3 downloads of talks by Cheri.

Cheri's Practice Blog

Follow "Cheri Huber's Practice Blog"
at http://cherispracticeblog.blogspot.com

There Is Nothing Wrong With You
An Extraordinary Eight-Day Retreat
based on the book
There Is Nothing Wrong With You: Going Beyond Self-Hate
by Cheri Huber

Inside each of us is a "persistent voice of discontent." It is constantly critical of life, the world, and almost everything we say and do. As children, in order to survive, we learned to listen to this voice and believe what it says.

This retreat is eight days of looking directly at how we are rejected and punished by the voices of self-hate and discovering how to let that go. Through a variety of exercises and periods of group processing, participants gain a clearer perspective on how they live their lives and on how to find compassion for themselves and others.

This work is challenging, joyous, fulfilling, scary, courageous, demanding, freeing, loving, kind, and compassionate—compassionate toward yourself and everyone you will ever know.

For information on attending contact:
Living Compassion/Zen Monastery Peace Center
P.O. Box 1756
Murphys, CA 95247
Ph.: 209-728-0860
Email: information@livingcompassion.org
Website: www.livingcompassion.org

ZEN MONASTERY PEACE CENTER

For a schedule of workshops and retreats and a list of meditation groups, contact us in one of the following ways.

Website: www.livingcompassion.org
Email: information@livingcompassion.org
Telephone: 209-728-0860

Zen Monastery Peace Center
P.O. Box 1756
Murphys, CA 95247

* * *

AFRICA VULNERABLE CHILDREN PROJECT

To find out about our work in an impoverished community in Zambia, visit www.livingcompassion.org.